HEROIC – EMPOWERED – RESILIENT

PURSUE HER

LIVING BOLDLY AS A DAUGHTER OF GOD

WORKBOOK WITH VIDEO ACCESS

Kelley J Bell

KELLEY BELL CONSULTING, LLC ®

Pursue HER ®
Living Boldly as a Daughter of God – Workbook with Video Access

Copyright © 2024 by Kelley J Bell

Printed in the United States of America. All rights reserved. No part of this book may be reproduced or transmitted in any form or by any means, electronic or mechanical, including photocopying and recording, or by any information storage and retrieval system, without permission in writing from the publisher.

Cover photography by: Kayla L. Smith

Kelley Bell Consulting, LLC ®
www.kbconsultingforher.com

I dedicate this book to you.

To the woman who believes in the God of Abraham, Isaac, and Jacob
To the woman who loves God and desires a closer walk with Him
To the woman who is open-minded and willing to invest in herself and do whatever it takes to walk in her God-given purpose.

Table of Contents

Introduction..vii

SECTION ONE
Heroic..1

Chapter 1: Being Heroic
Chapter 2: Being a Daughter of God
Chapter 3: Walking in Kingdom Authority

SECTION TWO
Empowered...23

Chapter 4: Being Empowered
Chapter 5 - Who is the Real You?

SECTION THREE
Resilient..47

Chapter Six - Being Resilient
Chapter Seven - Dying to Your Flesh

Section Four
Living as HER..71

    Chapter Eight - Balancing Life as HER
    Chapter Nine - Being HER as a Wife
    Chapter Ten - Being HER as a Mother
    Chapter Eleven - Being HER as a Ministry Leader
    Chapter Twelve - God Wants To Use You

Answer Key..95

Additional Resources...97

Introduction

Scan for a word from the author *before* reading the written introduction.

Living boldly as a daughter of God is an intentional process. Change will not happen in a person's life by only reading a book. That person must incorporate the work needed to achieve their desired result. In this case, you desire to live life boldly as a daughter of God. The title purposely has the word pursue in it, as you have to be actively engaged in order to achieve the goal of being heroic, empowered, and resilient.

Be honest and ask yourself, "How much energy will you give to achieve your goal?" I once had the opportunity to hear Les Brown speak. He said, "When you are born, you look like your parents. When you die, you look like your choices".

You have the power to change your life and it starts with your mindset and your determination to make a change.

This workbook aims to help you identify areas of your life that you need to work on so you can move toward your goal. I recommend that you use this workbook as a companion to the book *Pursue HER, Living Life Boldly as a Daughter of God* so that certain statements and questions will make more sense.

Throughout this workbook, there are spaces available for you to keep track of notes, "aha" moments you have encountered while reading the book, and answers to self-reflective questions that align with the topics and strategies discussed in each chapter.

I pray that every daughter of God gets to the place of full confidence in who they are in God. I pray that every daughter of God walks in their royal position according to God's view of them and their authority. You have the power to shift atmospheres and to make a positive change in your life and others. You can spread the news of Jesus to those around you so they, too, may also experience the freedom that God wants them to have.

In the notes section for each chapter of the book, take notes on different emotions or triggers that may arise while reading. If you read something that bothers you, write down what was said and identify the emotion you felt. Identifying your emotions is important to identify things that need to be addressed in your life. Things are often embedded in our subconscious, and we aren't aware of why we respond in certain ways or that there is a concern to address. I pray that God begins to reveal matters that may not be at the forefront of your mind but are suppressed or repressed so you may get to the root of your issues.

Getting to the root of your issues is imperative. Consider this example.

Quick disclaimer: I am not a physician or advising you to take medical advice from this book. Please consult with your doctor about any medical decisions before changing your health regimen.

If someone has high blood pressure, it's easy to go to the doctor and take a pill to help lower it. High blood pressure is a symptom of what's happening inside your body. The use of the pill is to help decrease the symptoms from manifesting. The root issue of someone having high blood pressure could be that they are overweight or their diet is causing the issue. If the person loses weight and changes their diet, which could address the root issue, they may be able to regulate their high blood pressure and possibly not need pills.

Here is another way of looking at the root issues. Let's say you are a woman that is addicted to watching porn. *Yeah, I went there.* Take the time to figure out why you are drawn to that. Is it because someone told you that was needed to become aroused? Is it because you have equated your value and worth as a woman based on sexual encounters and need to watch those videos to learn different ways to perform in the bedroom? Watching porn can be a symptom of a root issue that has not been addressed. Once you can get to the root, you can address it accordingly.

A true heart transformation will not occur if you don't get to the cause of certain actions, thoughts, and beliefs. As we address the root issues of our lives, we will minimize the symptoms that manifest.

Getting to root issues is not always fun. It can bring up hurtful memories and things you don't want to discuss. However, I recommend getting additional support from licensed or certified professionals to assist you in this process.

If you do not have a licensed counselor or life coach to guide you through your self-reflection process, I recommend finding one who can assist. I am familiar with the advice of going to the church's pastor for counseling. In my opinion, not all Pastors can provide effective counseling. I will be honest and don't mean to offend anyone, but the most damaging counseling I have had was from a Pastor.

Pastors are great for spiritual guidance, discussions about expounding on the biblical text, and providing emotional support.

However, be mindful and cautious of those without professional training to counsel individuals.

Licensed counselors are taught a series of processes and techniques that can help one deal with aspects of the brain, how to deal with trauma, and how to address issues at the root. If people don't deal with the root of their issues, the symptoms of those issues will show throughout life.

Even though Certified Life Coaches can address the root of issues, some do not but can provide guidance and support to get a person closer to their goals. Sometimes, a life coach may recommend a person speak with a counselor before using their services if they have identified that the potential client is dealing with deeper issues. Let's put it like this: a counselor is like a doctor. You go to them to figure out what is wrong with you and they help you address that problem. In contrast, a life coach is like a personal trainer. A person gets a personal trainer to help them reach a specific goal. The personal trainer didn't give them that goal, but they know the steps and provide the motivation needed to get that person to where they want to go.

I know these support levels include a financial fee; however, counseling agencies and sometimes opportunities through your employer will provide a limited number of counseling sessions for a small fee or no fee.

I mention those resources as pursuing HER is a lifelong process that may cause each person to utilize a variety of levels of support. As you do the work on yourself, there will be different seasons of your life where more work may be needed. It is all a part of the journey. This journal is here to be a guide throughout your journey. I encourage you to return to these exercises during different seasons of your life. As long as you have breath, there will always be something to work on.

It's time to do the work!

Section One

Heroic

Chapter 1: Being Heroic

Chapter 2: Being a Daughter of God

Chapter 3: Walking in Kingdom Authority

Scan for a word from the author *before* reading Section One of the book. (1-1)

Use the space below to write notes as you read Section One. Notes can include (but not limited to) questions and information that resonates with you.

NOTES

NOTES

NOTES

NOTES

NOTES

NOTES

NOTES

NOTES

> "The Holy Spirit serves many purposes in our lives."

NOTES

NOTES

NOTES

Scan for a word from the author *after* reading Section One of the book. (1-2)

Using the graphic organizer below, write the names of women you consider Heroic.

After listing names, explain why you consider those women to be heroic.

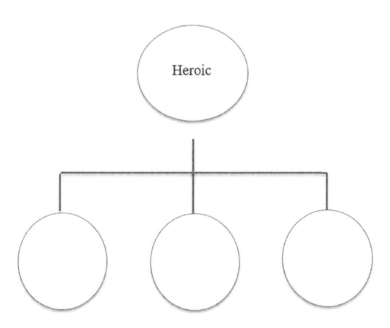

Person 1:

_____
_____
_____
_____
_____
_____

Person 2:

_____
_____
_____
_____
_____
_____

Person 3:

_____
_____
_____
_____
_____
_____

Scan for a word from the author *before answering the following questions.* (1-3)

1. In what ways have you shown that you were heroic?

_____

_____

_____

_____

_____

_____

2. Are there areas of improvement you need to work on regarding being heroic? If so, why do you think so, and what are those areas?

_____

_____

_____

_____

_____

_____

Scan for a word from the author *before* answering question number three. (1-4)

3. Take one of the areas listed above and identify steps you can take to move toward being heroic in that area.

_____
_____
_____
_____
_____
_____

Scan for a word from the author *before* answering the following questions. (1-5)

4. Have you been taught you have power as a daughter of God?

_____

5. If you have been taught that you have power as a daughter of God, how have you demonstrated that in your life?

_____

_____

_____

_____

_____

6. If you have not been taught that you have power as a daughter of God, how will you learn more about the power God has given you?

_____

_____

_____

_____

_____

7. Were any concepts shared in Chapter Two or Chapter Three contradictory to previous teachings you have received?

_____

_____

_____

If so, list the concepts that you need clarification on.

- _____
  _____
  _____
  _____

- _____
  _____
  _____
  _____

- _____
  _____
  _____
  _____

Make sure to take the time to cross-reference the concepts you have listed above with scriptures. Correctly studying and interpreting scriptures is imperative. Utilizing the assistance of a trusted spiritual mentor or influence may also be helpful when clarifying the concepts listed above.

8. Using the T-Chart below, acknowledge the areas you feel strong in your walk with Christ and the areas you would like to improve. On the left side, you will list the areas where you feel strong. You will list the areas you want to improve on the right side.

Example: STRONG: Consistent prayer life, Set Devotion Times

IMPROVE: Prayer life, Increasing my faith

STRONG	IMPROVE

9. Are you guilty of living a life of condemnation and fear due to mistakes you have made?

_____

10. What does the Bible say about living life with condemnation and fear? Identify scriptures to support your answer.

_____
_____
_____
_____
_____
_____

11. Have you equated your engagement in local church opportunities to have a close relationship with God?

_____

If so, why and how will you adjust this area?

_____
_____
_____
_____
_____

12. What should be the determining factor of having a close relationship with God?

_____
_____
_____
_____
_____
_____

13. In what ways can you operate in your Kingdom authority?

_____
_____
_____
_____
_____
_____

Scan a word from the author *before* going to Section Two. (1-6)

Section Two

Empowered

Chapter 4: Being Empowered

Chapter 5 - Who is the Real You?

Scan for a word from the author *before* reading Section Two of the book. (2-1)

Use the space below to write notes as you read Section Two. Notes can include (but not limited to) questions and information that resonates with you.

NOTES

NOTES

NOTES

NOTES

NOTES

NOTES

NOTES

NOTES

> "Are you living in the fullness of life or living guarded

NOTES

NOTES

NOTES

Scan a word from the author *after* reading Section Two of the book. (2-2)

1. In your opinion, list six characteristics of an empowered woman.

_____   _____

_____   _____

_____   _____

2. From the abovementioned characteristics, which of these characteristics do you have?

_____   _____

_____   _____

_____   _____

3. Which of the characteristics listed above do you desire to have?

_____   _____

_____   _____

_____   _____

4. Do you consider yourself to be empowered? Why or why not?

_____
_____
_____
_____
_____

5. If you do not consider yourself empowered, what do you think caused this feeling?

_____
_____
_____
_____
_____

6. What steps can you put in place to work on this area?

Step 1:

_____
_____
_____
_____

Step 2:

Step 3:

7. If you feel yourself empowered, what do you think caused this?

8. How can the Holy Spirit help you in your life? (Identify scriptures to support your answer.)

9. Why did God give His children access to the Holy Spirit? (Identify scriptures to support your answer.)

_____
_____
_____
_____
_____
_____

10. What are some ways that you can rely on the Holy Spirit?

_____
_____
_____
_____
_____

Scan a word from the author *after* completing question ten. (2-3)

Scan a word from the author *before* completing the next set of questions. (2-4)

As we begin the journey of discovering your true self, take a moment to reflect on what brings you joy and what triggers you. Use the organizers below to identify these important aspects of your life and fill in the boxes surrounding the identified words.

When identifying the things that trigger you, keep in mind these are the things that may need further processing with a counselor or life coach.

	TRIGGERS	

	BRINGS JOY	

1. Who is _____ (Enter your name)

_____
_____
_____
_____
_____

2. Do you believe that your roles and responsibilities define who you are? Why or why not?

_____
_____
_____
_____
_____

3. As a result of life experiences, what kind of woman have you become?

_____
_____
_____
_____
_____

4. What steps have you taken to deal with previous hurt, unpleasant life experiences, and trauma?

_____
_____
_____
_____

5. Can you identify any defense mechanisms that you use to protect yourself? If so, list what they are.

_____
_____
_____
_____

6. What are aspects of yourself that you would like to improve? (Example: stop procrastinating, be more secure in myself, have a positive mindset)

_____
_____
_____
_____
_____

7. What life experiences have you healed from?

_____
_____
_____
_____
_____

8. What life experiences do you need to heal from?

_____
_____
_____
_____
_____

9. When was the last time you asked God to show you - you?
_____
_____
_____
_____

- If you have, what did He show you, and how did you work on those areas?
_____
_____
_____
_____

- If you have not, do you have an open mind to ask Him and receive what He shows you?_____

  When you are ready, I encourage you to ask Him.

10. Using all the information you have gathered in this workbook, write 3-4 sentences describing the kind of woman you desire to be.
_____
_____
_____
_____
_____

Scan a word from the author *after* completing question twelve. (2-5)

Bonus Activity: If you could go to sleep and wake up and life could be exactly how you desired, how would your day go?

For this answer, dream big and write down every detail that comes to mind. Don't think about what is realistic or reasonable. I want you to dream with no inhibitions. Before writing your response, please close your eyes, imagine it, and verbalize how your day will go. Think about it from the moment you wake up. What kind of house would you wake up in? What color is the decor in your room? What type of job would you have? Think about your entire day. After you say it out loud, write down what you said.

The purpose of this question is to get you to continue to dream. I want you to stop for a moment from thinking about what you must do and think about what you desire to do. The desires you have in your heart are not by accident. Take what you have written down, share it with the Lord, and discuss it with Him.

_____
_____
_____
_____
_____

Section Three

Resilient

Chapter Six - Being Resilient

Chapter Seven - Dying to Your Flesh

Scan for a word from the author *before* reading Section Three of the book. (3-1)

Use the space below to write notes as you read Section Two. Notes can include (but not limited to) questions and information that resonates with you.

NOTES

NOTES

NOTES

NOTES

NOTES

NOTES

NOTES

NOTES

> "In the process of finding myself, this also meant dealing with the aspects of myself that are not pleasing to God."

NOTES

NOTES

NOTES

Scan for a word from the author *after* reading Section Three. (3-2)

1. If those close to you would describe how you respond when life challenges arise, what would they say?

_____
_____
_____
_____

2. How do you think you respond when life challenges arise?

_____
_____
_____
_____

3. In your own words, how do you define resiliency?

_____
_____
_____
_____

4. Do you believe you are resilient? Why or why not?

_____
_____
_____
_____
_____

5. Using the guide below, identify three women in the Bible who displayed resiliency.

Name:_____

Where in the Bible is her story located?

_____
_____
_____

What challenge did she have to overcome?

_____
_____
_____
_____

How did she show resiliency?
_____
_____
_____
_____

How were others impacted by her resiliency?
_____
_____
_____
_____

What can you learn from her display of resiliency?
_____
_____
_____
_____

Name:_____

Where in the Bible is her story located?
_____
_____
_____

What challenge did she have to overcome?

___
___
___
___
___

How did she show resiliency?

___
___
___
___
___

How were others impacted by her resiliency?

___
___
___
___
___

What can you learn from her display of resiliency?

_____
_____
_____
_____
_____
_____
_____

Name:_____

Where in the Bible is her story located?

_____
_____
_____

What challenge did she have to overcome?

_____
_____
_____
_____
_____
_____
_____

How did she show resiliency?

_____
_____
_____
_____
_____

How were others impacted by her resiliency?

_____
_____
_____
_____
_____

What can you learn from her display of resiliency?

_____
_____
_____
_____
_____

Scan for a word from the author *before* compleing the following questions. (3-3)

6. How have you been taught to deal with sin in your life?

_____
_____
_____
_____
_____
_____

7. Do you have a desire to live a life that is pleasing to God? Why or why not?

_____
_____
_____
_____
_____
_____

8. Are you willing to surrender every part of your life to God? Why or why not?

_____
_____
_____
_____
_____

9. How can you surrender your life to God?

_____
_____
_____
_____
_____

10. How many accountability partners/friends do you have that will redirect you to living life based on a biblical worldview?

_____
_____
_____
_____

Creating a circle of people that will help you in this area is imperative.

11. Have your actions to satisfy your fleshly desires stopped you from choosing to build a closer relationship with God? If so, why?

_____
_____
_____
_____

12. Do you believe that God wants a relationship with you while you are in the process of crucifying your flesh?

_____
_____

Write 2-3 scriptures that support your response.
Scripture 1:

_____
_____

Scripture 2:

_____
_____

Scripture 3:

_____
_____

Read about each person listed below using your Bible and answer the questions. Each person below went through a process of crucifying their flesh. As a result of their heart toward God and the decision to repent, they were used for the Kingdom of God. As you complete this task, I pray that God reveals truths that correlate with your life. Each person listed below was in different places in their lives and walked with God, yet God still had a purpose for them, and they chose to surrender to God.

King David - *1 Samuel and 2 Samuel*

1. What sins did David partake in?

_____

_____

2. What pleased God about David?

_____

_____

3. Did God forgive David?

_____

_____

4. How did God use David?

_____

_____

Apostle Paul (formerly known as Saul of Tarsus) - *Acts*

1. What sins did Saul partake in?
_____
_____

2. What happened on the Road of Damascus?
_____
_____

3. Did Saul consider his actions against Christians as sin before His road of Damascus experience?
_____
_____

4. Why did God change Saul's name to Paul?
_____
_____

5. Did God forgive Paul?
_____
_____

6. How did God use Paul?
_____
_____

Rahab - *Joshua*

1. When Rahab is introduced in the book of Joshua, what was her "occupation"?

_____

_____

2. How did Rahab help the people of God?

_____

_____

3. Despite her sin, Rahab had much F __ __ __ h. (Fill in the blank)

_____

_____

4. How is Rahab related to King David and Jesus?

_____

_____

Scan a word from the author *before* going to the next section. (3-4)

Section Four

Living as HER

Chapter Eight - Balancing Life as HER

Chapter Nine - Being HER as a Wife

Chapter Ten - Being HER as a Mother

Chapter Eleven - Being HER as a Ministry Leader

Chapter Twelve - God Wants To Use You

Scan a word from the author *before* reading Section Four of the book. (4-1)

Use the space below to write notes as you read Section Four. Notes can include (but not limited to) questions and information that resonates with you.

NOTES

NOTES

NOTES

NOTES

NOTES

NOTES

NOTES

NOTES

NOTES

NOTES

NOTES

NOTES

> "Do not forget that your role as a daughter of God is critical to your effectiveness in every aspect of your life.

NOTES

NOTES

NOTES

Scan a word from the author *after* reading Section 4. (4-2)

1. What kind of calendar will you use?

_____

_____

_____

_____

2. Will you schedule on a weekly, bi-weekly, or monthly routine?

_____

_____

_____

_____

3. What day will you begin implementing this strategy?

_____

_____

_____

_____

Scan a word from the author *before* completing the next activity.
(4-3)

4. Create a list of all your current roles. Next to each role, identify how you show up as a daughter of God first in that area of your life.

Examples of roles: Wife, Mother, Employee, Entrepreneur, Ministry Leader, Sister, Friend, Mentor, Mentee, Girlfriend, Volunteer,

If you identify areas where improvement is needed, ask God to show you how. You may also use any tips provided in the book as a guide.

Example:
Role: Teacher
Daughter of God: Ask God to help create lesson plans, pray for co-workers, students, and safety on campus

Role:_____

Daughter of God:_____

_____

Role:_____

Daughter of God:_____

_____

Role:_____

Daughter of God:_____

_____

Role:_____

Daughter of God:_____

_____

Role:_____

Daughter of God:_____

_____

Role:_____

Daughter of God:_____

_____

Role:_____

Daughter of God:_____

_____

Role:_____

Daughter of God:_____

_____

Role:_____

Daughter of God:_____

_____

Role:_____

Daughter of God:_____

_____

Role:_____

Daughter of God:_____

_____

Role:_____

Daughter of God:_____

_____

Role:_____

Daughter of God:_____

_____

Scan a word from the author *before* going to the next section. (4-4)

5. What will you do with what you have just read?

_____
_____
_____
_____
_____
_____

6. What will you do with the suppressed feelings, thoughts, and experiences?

_____
_____
_____
_____
_____

7. How will you balance your responsibilities while staying rooted in your role as a daughter of God?

_____
_____
_____
_____
_____

8. Has God revealed how He wants to use you for His glory? If so, write out what He has told you.

_____
_____
_____
_____
_____

9. If you are unsure how God wants to use you, do you desire to be used by God?

_____

_____

If your answer is yes, your next step is to continue to develop or strengthen your relationship with God by spending time with Him and learning more about Him. Identifying current passions in your life is a start. Next, identify why you love doing it, which indicates your purpose. Walking in your purpose will not be selfish and add value to others.

If your answer is no, explain why you do not want to be used by God. Be detailed in your response to get to the root reason for your answer.

_____

_____

_____

_____

_____

10. What changes will you make to live boldly as a daughter of God?

_____

_____

_____

_____

Scan for a final word from the author. (4-5)

Answer Key

Section Three -

King David

Books of 1 Samuel and 2 Samuel

1. What sins did David partake in? *Adultery, Murder, Deception*

2. What pleased God about David? *His Heart*

3. Did God forgive David? *Yes*

4. How did God use David? *David created a lineage from which Jesus Christ was to be born.*

Apostle Paul (also known as Saul of Tarsus)

Book of Acts

1. What sins did Saul partake in? *(Murdered and persecuted Christians)*

2. What happened on the Road of Damascus? *He encountered Jesus, who took his eyesight and gave him specific directions on what to do next.*

3. Did Saul consider his actions against Christians as sin before His road of Damascus experience? *No*

4. Did God forgive Saul? *Yes*

5. How did God use Paul? *He wrote many letters in the New Testament to share the gospel of Jesus.*

Rahab

Book of Joshua

1. When Rahab is introduced in the book of Joshua, what was her "occupation"? *Prostitute*

2. How did Rahab help the people of God? *Hid the spies and helped them escape.*

3. Despite her sin, Rahab had much <u>*Faith*</u>

4. How is Rahab related to King David and Jesus? *King David and Jesus were descendants of Rahab.*

Are you ready for additional resources?

God's Marriage or My Marriage is a testimonial experience of a wife who created a marriage that she desired and a pleasing marriage to God. By applying biblical principles and practical relationship skills, she was able to transform her marriage! Are you ready to learn how to combine foundational principles of marriage with practical relationship skills or learn how to successfully navigate the journey of marriage while regaining or maintaining control of your emotions? Then this book is for you. This book also includes self-reflective questions after each chapter to implement further the strategies taught. Marriage takes the work of two, but you can only control yourself! Learn how today!

Also available in Spanish

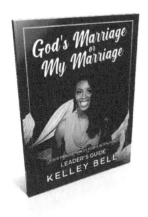

Are you ready to take your small group discussions to the next level? Then **God's Marriage or My Marriage Leader's Guide** is the perfect resource to help you accomplish this goal. With this guide, get ready to incorporate research-based instructional strategies into your small group setting, receive detailed lesson plans for each session, and access lesson ideas for virtual and face-to-face sessions. In addition, this guide allows you to take your participants through a transformational process that equips them with the steps to apply what they have learned to their marriages.

God's Marriage or My Marriage Online Course is a powerful course to transform your mindset and create a marriage aligned with God's Intention. Through Kelley's transparency and sincere passion for helping women, she can connect with her audience and create a safe space in this course.

Once completing this course, you will never look at your marriage the same again!

GOD'S MARRIAGE OR MY MARRIAGE

- LIFE TIME ACCESS
- SELF-PACED
- AFFORDABLE

Kelley J. Bell
Family Consultant

REGISTER NOW
www.kbconsultingforher.com

Pursue HER Podcast is for women juggling multiple roles and seeking strategies to balance it all. Kelley specializes in teaching women to combine biblical principles and practical strategies to guide them through their life journey. She has created a space for women to embrace their journey by sharing her journey! It's time for a little talk! Will you join her?

Raising Kingdom-Minded Children is a step-by-step guide that teaches parents to combine biblical principles and practical parenting skills. The journey of parenthood can be challenging, but with the proper guidance and support, it can be pretty fulfilling!

In this guide, you will learn proven tips and strategies to implement in your parenting journey. Kelley teaches you how to build upon your strengths as a parent and improve in the needed areas.

Let's do this together, no matter where you are on your journey!

Pursue HER Life Coaching is a method Kelley Bell Consulting uses that consists of several actionable steps women will take to create the best version of themselves. If you are a mother, wife, or wife-to-be, you will learn to be Heroic, Empowered, and Resilient within those roles.

If you do not identify with the above roles but want assistance navigating your life as a daughter of God, Pursue HER Coaching is also for you!

Visit **www.kbconsultingforher.com** for details on resources

HAVE QUESTIONS?
info@kbconsultingforher.com

Made in the USA
Middletown, DE
01 September 2024

60288276R00066